Spooky
MATH

More or Less
and a Vampire's Guess

by Spencer Brinker

Consultant:
Kimberly Brenneman, PhD
National Institute for Early Education Research
Rutgers University
New Brunswick, New Jersey

BEARPORT
PUBLISHING

New York, New York

Credits

Publisher: Kenn Goin
Editorial Director: Adam Siegel
Senior Editor: Joyce Tavolacci
Creative Director: Spencer Brinker
Photo Illustrations: Kim Jones and Bearport Publishing

Library of Congress Cataloging-in-Publication Data

Brinker, Spencer, author.
   More or less and a vampire's guess / by Spencer Brinker ; consultant: Kimberly
Brenneman, PhD, National Institute for Early Education Research, Rutgers University, New
Brunswick, New Jersey.
       pages cm. — (Spooky math)
   Audience: Ages 4–8.
   Includes bibliographical references and index.
   ISBN-13: 978-1-62724-330-8 (library binding)
   ISBN-10: 1-62724-330-5 (library binding)
   1. Counting—Juvenile literature. 2. Arithmetic—Juvenile literature. 3. Vampires—Juvenile
literature. I. Title.
   QA113.B6874 2015
   513.2'11—dc23
                                    2014012031

For more information, write to Bearport Publishing Company, Inc., 45 West 21st Street,
Suite 3B, New York, New York 10010. Printed in the United States of America.

10 9 8 7 6 5 4 3 2 1

Contents

More or Less?

Welcome my friend!
Please pull up a chair.

I'm sorting through items.
Come help me compare.

Lots of my things
are a bit of a mess.

How can I tell which are more, which are less?

Sometimes I count and sometimes I guess!

Which has more owls,
the wall or the tree?

To find out is easy.
Let's count them and see.

6

ANSWER: The tree has more owls. There are three owls on the tree and two on the wall.

Green crocs and red snakes slither onto the floor.

10

Count them and tell me which toilet holds more.

My Halloween table's a feast for the eyes.

Count to see if there are more pumpkins or pies.

ANSWER: There are more pumpkins. There are six pumpkins and five pumpkin pies.

My nails are not pretty.
Some are green. Some are blue.

I think more are green.
Count them. Is it true?

ANSWER: There are more green fingernails.
There are six green fingernails.

I love gardens at night.
The sun's bad for my skin.

Which plant has more moonberries, the thick or the thin?

17

There are spiders on my table.
There are spiders on my door.

There are spiders on my ceiling.
Which hiding place has more?

19

Which group has fewer,
and which group has more?

The mice resting on the pillow,
or the rats dancing on the floor?

ANSWER: There are fewer mice than rats. There are four mice on the pillow and five rats on the floor.

There are more toads than coffins,
I'm sure you'll agree.

Just how many more?
Let's count them and see.

ANSWER: There are four more toads than coffins.
There are three coffins and seven toads.

I have bugs in two jars.
Which jar holds less?

To find out the answer, don't count, just guess!

In my mouth you will see
lots of teeth can be found.

Are there more pointy teeth—
or more teeth that are round?

ANSWER: There are more round teeth.

My neighbors wear scarves. "We're so cold," they both say.

Which scarf has more stripes, the blue or the gray?

Which place has more bats, the sky or the tree?

ANSWER: There are more bats flying in the sky. There are ten bats in the sky.

One final question:
Can you find *me*?

Read More

Capote, Lori. *Monster Knows More Than, Less Than.* North Mankato, MN: Capstone (2013).

Mattern, Joanne. *More Than, Less Than (Little World Math Concepts).* Vero Beach, FL: Rourke (2011).

Learn More Online

To learn more about comparing numbers, visit **www.bearportpublishing.com/SpookyMath**

About the Author

Spencer Brinker lives and works in New York City, where there are more taxis than subway trains. He can easily guess that there are more people than either taxis or trains. His fingernails are neither green nor blue.